POPE FRANCIS

FIRST POPE FROM THE AMERICAS

POPE FRANCIS

FIRST POPE FROM THE AMERICAS

STEPHANIE WATSON

LERNER PUBLICATIONS COMPANY • MINNEAPOLIS

For Mary Katherine, who broadened my world view on religion

Lerner Publications Company
A division of Lerner Publishing Group, Inc.
241 First Avenue North
Minneapolis, MN U.S.A. 55401

Website address: www.lernerbooks.com

The images in this book are used with the permission of: © Peter Macdiarmid/Getty Images, pp. 2, 31; © Christopher Furlong/Getty Images, p. 6; © Stefano Costantino/Demotix/CORBIS, p. 8; © Jeff J Mitchell/Getty Images, p. 9; © Courtesy of Maria Elena Bergoglio/Handout/Reuters/ Corbis, p. 11; © AFP/Getty Images, p. 12; © Franco Origlia/Jesuit General Curia via Getty Images, p. 13; © Peter Paul Rubens/The Bridgeman Art Library/Getty Images, p. 14; AP Photo/ Eduardo DiBaia, p. 17; REUTERS/Enrique Marcarian, p. 18; AP Photo/Pablo Leguizamon, p. 19; © Parroquia Virgen de Caacupe/Handout/Reuters/Corbis, p. 20; AP Photo/Buenos Aires Archbishop Office, p. 21; © Enrique Garcia Medina/Reuters/CORBIS, p. 22; © ARTURO MARI/ AFP/Getty Images, p. 24; AP Photo/Daniel Luna, p. 25; © JUAN MABROMATA/AFP/Getty Images, p. 26; © OSSERVATORE ROMANO/Reuters/Corbis, p. 27; © Michael Loccisano/Getty Images, p. 28; © DeAgostini/Getty Images, p. 29; © STEFANO RELLANDINI/Reuters/Corbis, p. 32; © AFP PHOTO/OSSERVATORE ROMANO/Getty Images, p. 35; © Franco Origlia/Getty Images, p. 36; AP Photo/L'Osservatore Romano, HO, pp. 37, 38, 39.

Front Cover: © FILIPPO MONTEFORTE/AFP/Getty Images.

Main body text set in Rotis Serif Std 55 Regular 13.5/17. Typeface provided by Adobe Systems.

Library of Congress Cataloging-in-Publication Data

Watson, Stephanie, 1969–
    Pope Francis : first pope from the Americas / Stephanie Watson.
        p.   cm. — (Gateway biographies)
    Includes index.
    ISBN 978-1-4677-2176-9 (lib. bdg. : alk. paper)
    ISBN 978-1-4677-2186-8 (eBook)
    1. Francis, Pope, 1936– —Juvenile literature. 2. Popes—Biography—Juvenile literature. I.
Title.
    BX1378.7.W38 2014
    282.092—dc23 [B]   2013013761

Manufactured in the United States of America
1 – BP – 7/15/13

CONTENTS

White smoke rises from the chimney of the Sistine Chapel on March 13, 2013.

It was the night of March 13, 2013. Darkness had fallen over Saint Peter's Square, a large plaza that sits in front of Saint Peter's Basilica in Vatican City. Vatican City is an independent city-state within the city of Rome, Italy. Vatican City is home to the Catholic Church, the world's largest Christian church.

In the square, more than one hundred thousand people huddled together under umbrellas against the cold and steadily falling rain. Many of them had been waiting there all day. They did not seem to mind the cold or the darkness. They were focused on one point—the chimney of the Sistine Chapel. The Sistine Chapel is home to the Catholic Church's leader, the pope.

At 7:05 P.M. local time, puffs of white smoke plumed from the chimney. The smoke was just what the crowd had been waiting to see. It wasn't just any smoke—it was a signal. White smoke is the age-old way that the Catholic Church communicates its election of a new pope. The smoke comes from burning the ballots used to elect the pope.

The crowd erupted. They cheered. They waved flags from different countries—Brazil, Italy, the United States, and others. Amid all the excitement, one question was on everybody's mind: just who was the new pope who'd been elected that night? The crowd would have to wait and see.

Nearly an hour passed. Bands of musicians from the Vatican and the Italian military marched through the square and up the steps of Saint Peter's Basilica. Finally, there was movement from the balcony of the Basilica, high above the square. A thick red curtain parted. Three men appeared. In the middle was French cardinal Jean-Louis

An excited crowd awaits the announcement of the new pope after seeing white smoke rise from the Sistine Chapel on March 13, 2013.

Tauran. In a voice shaky with emotion, he announced in Latin, "Habemus Papam." (We have a pope.)

Then he told the crowd the name of the new pope—Jorge Mario Bergoglio of Argentina. He would be known as Pope Francis. That was the new name he'd chosen as part of his election to the papacy. Pope Francis stepped to the front of the balcony. He was dressed simply in white papal robes, not the red cape and large gold cross popes usually wear. The crowd again began to cheer. They shouted, "Viva il Papa!" (Long live the pope!) Some people wept.

Pope Francis *(second from left)* speaks to the crowd in Saint Peter's Square following his election as the 266th pope of the Roman Catholic Church.

It was a powerful moment—the election of the man who is considered to be one of the world's most important religious leaders. When Jorge was named pope, he took control of a religious flock that numbered 1.2 billion Catholics worldwide. Pope Francis became the 266th pope in the Catholic Church's two-thousand-year history. His election was notable for many reasons. He was the first pope from the Society of Jesuits. He was also one of the only popes in history to come from a country outside Europe. And he was the very first pope from Latin America.

Pope Francis was noteworthy for other reasons too. In some ways, he was very much like Pope Benedict who had come before him. He held firm to the church's traditional teachings. Pope Francis believed the Catholic Church should not change its policies to allow same-sex marriage, birth control, and female priests—changes that some critics of the traditional teachings had been calling for. Yet unlike Pope Benedict, he was a very simple, humble man. He had washed the feet of AIDS patients and championed the rights of the poor. It was clear from the start that this pope would leave his mark on his church—and on the world.

THE FUTURE POPE IS BORN

Jorge Mario Bergoglio, the man who would be pope, was born on December 17, 1936. His family lived in Buenos Aires, the capital of Argentina. Jorge's father, Mario Jose Bergoglio, had immigrated to Argentina from northern

Jorge Mario Bergoglio *(left)* poses with his brother Oscar after taking his first Holy Communion in 1942.

Italy. He worked on the railroad in his new country. Jorge's mother, Regina Maria Sivori, was a homemaker. Jorge was one of five children.

Jorge's two passions were soccer (called football in Argentina) and tango dancing. He played soccer every weekend. In addition, Jorge kept busy with his schoolwork. One school he attended was Wilfrid Barón de los Santos Angeles, a Catholic school in greater Buenos Aires. He was known as a serious student, although he also enjoyed spending time with friends and his close-knit family. Not

a lot is known about Jorge's early years, but his life both at home and in school appeared to be full, balanced, and happy.

In 1957, at the age of twenty-one, Bergoglio's peaceful life was disrupted when he came down with an infection in his lungs. Doctors had to remove part of one lung. Losing a piece of his lung did not affect Bergoglio's life for too long, however. He was still able to do most of the things everyone else can do—including go to school.

Bergoglio decided that he wanted to study science, a subject he'd always had an interest in. He graduated from the University of Buenos Aires with a master's degree in chemistry. But soon he found another calling. This calling took him back to the religious instruction he'd gotten in Catholic school as a boy. Jorge felt drawn to the study of Catholicism. Not only that—the young man felt that he was meant to join the clergy. In March 1958, he entered the seminary of Villa Devoto in Buenos Aires. There, he studied to be a priest. For many years, Bergoglio combined religious training and other sorts of education. He got a degree in philosophy from Colegio Máximo San José in San Miguel, a town about 25 miles (40 kilometers) north of Buenos Aires. In the mid-1960s, he taught literature and psychology to students at the Colegio del Salvador, a university in Buenos Aires.

In 1969 Bergoglio was ordained a Jesuit priest. He was thirty-two years old. Four years later, the Jesuits named him their Provincial of Argentina. In this position, he supervised all the Society of Jesuits' activities in Argentina.

This photograph from the 1960s was taken during Bergoglio's years teaching at the Colegio del Salvador.

WHO ARE THE JESUITS?

The Jesuits are members of the Society of Jesuits, the largest religious order of the Roman Catholic Church. The founder of this order was a Spanish military officer named Ignatius de Loyola. In 1521 Ignatius was defending a Spanish fortress against the French. During battle he was hit in the leg by a cannonball. While recovering from his injury, he began reading about the lives of Christian saints. He was so moved by what he read that he had a spiritual transformation. Ignatius devoted himself to a life of poverty, obedience, and devotion to the poor. These became the ideals of his followers. They called themselves the Jesuits.

Peter Paul Rubens painted this portrait of Ignatius de Loyola in the 1600s.

Today there are about seventeen thousand Jesuits around the world. They work with the poor and are patrons of the arts. They publish magazines, create works of art, and write music. And they run colleges, such as Georgetown University, Boston College, and Loyola University. The Jesuits are very loyal to the pope. But until Pope Francis was elected, a Jesuit had never served as pope.

CRUEL NEW LEADERS

In the mid-1970s, Bergoglio's career as a Jesuit leader was on the rise. However, his country was on the verge of turmoil. In 1974 Argentinian president Juan Perón died. His wife, Isabel Perón, stepped in to become the country's new president. However, she was a weak leader. On March 24, 1976, a military junta (group) led by General Jorge Rafael Videla seized power from Isabel Perón. This launched one of the most brutal periods in Argentina's history. Today, it is known as Argentina's "dirty war."

The new military government launched a campaign against anyone they thought disagreed with them. They kidnapped thousands of people and took them to secret detention centers. The military tortured or killed many of the people they kidnapped. These people became known as *los desaparecidos* (the disappeared).

During this time, many Jesuits became part of a movement called liberation theology. They encouraged the people of Argentina to fight back against poverty, injustice, and oppression. Even though Bergoglio wanted to help the poor, he was against liberation theology. He felt that it was based on the ideas of Communism. People who follow this political movement believe there should be no social classes and everyone should share what they earn. The Catholic Church has long been opposed to the ideas of Communism.

In 1976 two Jesuit priests who followed liberation theology—Orlando Yorio and Francisco Jalics—were serving the poor in the slums of Buenos Aires. Members of the military regime came to the slums and kidnapped them. For five months, these two men were held at a military camp.

The two priests had served under Bergoglio. Many people accused the provincial of failing to protect the two men in his charge. They claimed Bergoglio was on the side of the brutal military leaders. "He turned priests in during the dictatorship," accused Argentinian journalist Horacio Verbitsky.

Yet Bergoglio said that he had done everything he could to protect the two priests. He said he had personally

THE BAD REVEREND

During the dirty war, many religious leaders fought back against the evil military rulers. However, at least one leader was on the side of the torturers and killers. He was the Reverend Christian von Wernich, former chaplain of the Buenos Aires police. (A chaplain is a religious leader who serves in a nonreligious place, such as a hospital, a police station, or a military unit.) During those dark days, Wernich was accused of helping torture and kill political prisoners for the military junta.

After the junta's rule ended, the Catholic Church helped Wernich leave Argentina and hide in Chile. But in 2003, he was brought back to Argentina and put on trial for his crimes. In 2007 he was sentenced to life in prison for seven killings, forty-two abductions, and thirty-four cases of torture.

asked dictator Jorge Videla to release Yorio and Jalics. Eventually the two men were let go. Bergoglio said he also hid people on church property to protect them from the military regime. Once he gave a man identity papers so he could escape from Argentina. "I believe he did all he could at that time," said Francesca Ambrogetti, who later wrote a biography about Jorge.

The military was eventually pushed out of power. But while they ruled, they kidnapped, tortured, and killed as many as thirty thousand people. In some people's minds, Bergoglio did not do enough to prevent the slaughter.

Women in Buenos Aires line up to vote for the first time in ten years as Argentina shifts from a military to a civilian government in 1983.

MINISTERING TO THE POOR

During the military regime, Bergoglio found himself at odds with other Jesuit leaders in Argentina. The other leaders were strongly against the military. And they thought Bergoglio was too agreeable to the dictators. In 1979 Bergoglio's term ended. The new provincial sent him to San Miguel to serve as the rector (the priest in charge) of the Jesuit school, Colegio Máximo, where he had studied about two decades earlier.

In 1986 he went to Germany to earn his doctorate in philosophy. A few months later, he returned to Buenos Aires to finish his studies, but the provincial again sent him away. This time, Bergoglio went to Córdoba—a town about six hours to the northwest of Buenos Aires.

There, he kept working on his doctorate.

After Bergoglio completed his doctorate, in 1992, Antonio Quarracino, Archbishop of Buenos Aires, called him back to the city. Quarracino named Bergoglio his auxiliary bishop. An auxiliary bishop is like an

Bergoglio worked closely with Antonio Quarracino *(left)* in Buenos Aires during the 1990s.

assistant who helps when there is too much work for the archbishop to handle alone. Bergoglio helped the bishop oversee the churches of Buenos Aires. He was also named Titular Bishop of Auca, a symbolic title for someone who is in charge of a diocese (religious district) that no longer exists.

On February 28, 1998, Bergoglio got another promotion. He became Archbishop of Buenos Aires, taking over from Quarracino. As archbishop, he could have lived in a big, elegant church mansion in Buenos Aires. Yet that was not his style. He preferred a humbler life, so he took a simple room downtown. He cooked his own meals. Instead of being driven around by a chauffeur, Bergoglio rode the bus or took the subway. When priests called for advice or

Bergoglio *(second from left)* was known for riding the subway in Buenos Aires. This photo is from 2008.

help, he always took the calls himself. He wrote down any complaints or requests in a little notebook he kept with him.

Bergoglio was often seen walking the streets of Buenos Aires. As he walked, he talked to people. He was very worried about his country's poor. He called Argentina "the most unequal part of the world." Bergoglio asked Argentina's government to give more social services to the poor.

More than 4 million of Buenos Aires's approximately 12 million people are poor. Many of them live in shantytowns. These slums are packed with rickety shacks and filled with garbage and pollution. They are unhealthful, dangerous places for people to live. As archbishop, Bergoglio often came to visit these towns. He walked through the crowded slums alone. Even though the

Bergoglio *(center)* celebrates Mass in a Buenos Aires slum in the late 1990s.

crime rate was high, he never brought a bodyguard along to protect him.

The archbishop also cared about military veterans of the Falklands war (1982). Argentina and Great Britain had fought this war over which country owned the rights to the Falkland Islands in the South Atlantic Ocean. About 650 Argentine and 255 British soldiers were killed during the war. Many more were injured. Bergoglio often had tea and talked with veterans of the war. "He has a huge heart," Argentine veteran Jorge Zamudio said of the archbishop.

THE HUMBLE CARDINAL

The Vatican noticed Bergoglio's piety and concern for his people. On February 21, 2001, Pope John Paul II named him cardinal. Cardinals are senior members of the Catholic Church in charge of electing a new pope when a former pope dies.

Pope John Paul II *(left)* embraces newly promoted Cardinal Jorge Mario Bergoglio in 2001.

Most cardinals wear bright red robes to show their position. Not Cardinal Bergoglio. "He never dresses like a cardinal," said Gregory James Venables, head of the Anglican Church in southern South America. "It's not to be scruffy. But that's his character. He is very, very, very humble."

That humility led him to perform simple acts that had a great impact on his patrons. In February 2001, while visiting Muñiz Hospital in Buenos Aires, he asked for a jar of water. Then he proceeded to wash the feet of patients with HIV—the virus that causes AIDS. Cardinal Bergoglio also kissed the patients' feet. He told reporters that "society forgets the sick and the poor."

During that same year, Bergoglio's concern for the poor was tested. Argentina fell into a deep financial crisis. The government owed billions of dollars to foreign countries

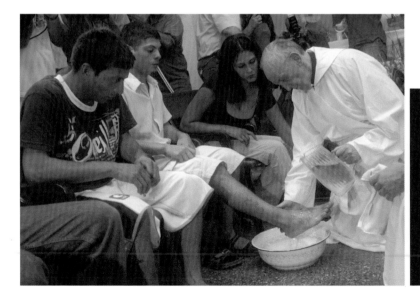

Bergoglio washes the feet of residents at a shelter for drug users in 2008.

that it could not pay back. To save money, the government cut jobs. Many people lost their wages. At the same time, prices in Argentina rose. During his homilies (sermons), Bergoglio denounced the corrupt politicians. He believed they had caused the crisis. He led talks between politicians and citizens' groups to help ease the money problems in his country. In 2003 the economy finally started to improve in Argentina.

ALMOST POPE

On April 2, 2005, Pope John Paul II died at the age of eighty-four. He had served as the head of the Catholic Church for more than twenty-five years. At his death, the cardinals knew they needed to elect a new pope. Bergoglio was one of the cardinals who met in Vatican City as part of the papal conclave—the group that elects a new pope.

During this conclave, the cardinals meet in the Sistine Chapel. They swear an oath of secrecy in Latin. Then they vote with a secret ballot. To be elected, a cardinal needs to get at least two-thirds of the vote. It often takes three, four, or even more ballots to get enough votes to elect one cardinal as pope.

As in any election, there are always a few front-runners for pope. These experienced cardinals uphold the teachings of the Catholic Church. In 2005 one of the front-runners was Bergoglio. But after four ballots, another cardinal—Joseph Ratzinger of Germany—was named the

Cardinals enter the Sistine Chapel for the papal conclave in 2005.

new pope. He took the name Pope Benedict XVI. Although Bergoglio was not elected pope in 2005, it would not be long before his name would come up again in a papal conclave.

THE TWO SIDES OF CARDINAL BERGOGLIO

On November 8, 2005, Bergoglio got another promotion. He was elected president of the Bishops' Conference of Argentina. In this position, he led all the bishops of his country. He worked with them on issues important to the church. Bergoglio held this position for two three-year terms.

Many people in Argentina loved Bergoglio. He continued to care for the sick and the poor. At times, he even took a stand against his own church for his people's rights. Bergoglio spoke out against priests in Buenos Aires who would not baptize (admit into the church) babies born to mothers who were not married. (Having a baby outside of marriage is traditionally considered wrong in the Catholic Church.) He accused those priests of hypocrisy—when a person says one thing but does another. He thought that men who spoke about compassion should show compassion to any mother who wanted to have her baby baptized.

Although he was well liked, Bergoglio sometimes clashed with the government of Argentina. At the time, the president was Néstor Kirchner. When his term ended in 2007, Kirchner's wife, Cristina Fernández de Kirchner, took over.

Cristina Fernández de Kirchner *(left)* and her husband, Néstor Kirchner, wave to the crowd after her swearing in as the country's first elected female president.

She became Argentina's first elected female president. Both Kirchners were very liberal. That means they were open to new ideas—ideas with which the Catholic Church did not always agree.

During their terms, the Kirchners made many changes in Argentina. They wanted to make it legal for people of the same sex to marry and adopt children. They offered free birth control to their people to prevent unwanted pregnancies. Bergoglio did not agree with these changes. He called same-sex marriage the devil's work and a "destructive attack on God's plan." He said that gay adoption discriminated against children. Cristina Fernández de Kirchner called his position "medieval." She was referring to medieval times, or the Middle Ages (about A.D. 500–1500), when people could be put to death for loving someone of the same sex.

Ernesto Larrese *(left)* and Alejandro Vannelli pose for photographers after getting married in 2010. The couple was one of the first to wed after Argentina legalized same-sex marriage.

THE POPE STEPS DOWN

In the Catholic Church, popes traditionally serve until their death. So it was a big surprise when Pope Benedict XVI announced on February 11, 2012, that he would resign. He was the first pope in six hundred years to do so.

The pope said he was stepping down because he was too old to finish his term. He was eighty-five years old. However, some people believed he stepped down because of some scandals that had erupted in the Catholic Church in recent years. One of those scandals involved the sexual abuse of children by priests. The Catholic Church was blamed for covering up the abuse and protecting the priests involved. Questions also arose about the way the

Pope Benedict XVI *(center)* announces his resignation during a meeting with cardinals on February 11, 2013.

U.S. Catholics protest outside of Saint Patrick's Cathedral on Easter in 2010.

Vatican bank handled money. There were rumors that the bank was being used to hide money for the Mafia—an organized crime group.

Yet another scandal erupted in January 2012. Pope Benedict's butler stole his personal papers, and a journalist published them. The papers detailed bribery, fraud, and other types of corruption in the church. That scandal became known as Vatileaks because the papers were leaked from the Vatican.

Pope Benedict XVI stepped down on February 28, 2013. As he left his job, the leaders of the church looked for a replacement. They knew they needed to choose someone who could reform the church. Many Catholics had grown tired of the scandals. They were leaving the church in large numbers. In 2008 alone, the number of Catholics in the United States had dropped by four hundred thousand.

A few cardinals were thought to be "papabile." This

means they were qualified to be pope. They included Cardinal Angelo Scola of Italy, Cardinal Marc Ouellet of Canada, Cardinal Odilo Scherer of Brazil, and Cardinal Timothy Dolan of the United States (New York). Bergoglio was among the cardinals considered. At the age of seventy-six, he was the oldest of the cardinals.

On Tuesday, March 12, the secret conclave of 115 cardinals began. One ballot was held that day. The next day, four more ballots were cast. In the fifth ballot, finally there were enough votes to choose a pope. Bergoglio received seventy-seven votes. He would be the new pope. The other cardinals applauded. When Cardinal Bergoglio accepted the position, many of them cried. His friend Cardinal Claudio Hummes hugged and kissed him. He told Bergoglio, "Don't forget the poor." This plea made the new pope think of Saint Francis of Assisi, a saint who had devoted his life to helping the poor. He decided that would be his name—Pope Francis.

This fifteenth-century illustration shows Saint Francis of Assisi.

PAPAL NAMES

Bergoglio was the first pope ever to take the name Francis. If another pope chooses that name in the future, then Bergoglio's name will change to Pope Francis I. The next pope to take the name will be known as Pope Francis II.

So far there has been only one Pope Francis. Here are a few papal names that have been more popular throughout history:

- John—21 popes
- Gregory—16 popes
- Benedict—16 popes
- Clement—14 popes
- Innocent—13 popes

MEET THE NEW POPE

Just moments after his name was announced, Pope Francis stepped out onto the balcony overlooking the waiting crowds in Saint Peter's Square. In Italian, with a faint Spanish accent, he began to speak. He thanked the people. Then he told the crowd, "Let us begin this journey together, this journey for the Roman Catholic Church. It's a journey of friendship and love and faith between us. Let us pray for one another, let us pray for all the world."

Usually the new pope would then bless the crowd. Not Pope Francis. He asked the crowd to bless *him*. He lowered

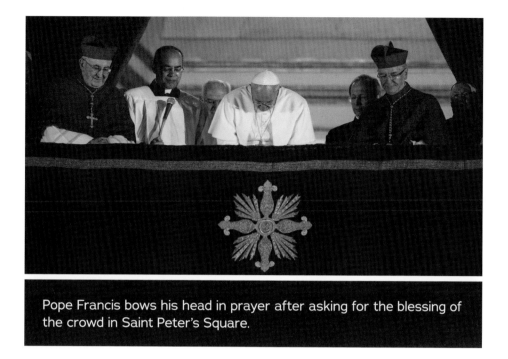

Pope Francis bows his head in prayer after asking for the blessing of the crowd in Saint Peter's Square.

his head in a sign of humility while the crowd did as he had asked. Then he said, "Let's pray for the world."

Other high-ranking members of the Catholic Church recognized Pope Francis's humble style. "He's a very simple man," said Luis R. Zarama, Auxiliary Bishop of Atlanta, Georgia. "It's very clear from the way he approached the people and asked them to bless him and pray for him. It's a beautiful sign of closeness and humility."

Praise for the new pope was widespread. "[He's] a man who calmly stands for what's right and just," said Cardinal Edward Egan, the Archbishop Emeritus (past Archbishop) of New York. Catholics also seemed to be pleased with the choice of a Jesuit pope who was born outside of Europe. "As a Catholic I'm really excited that they have made this break with tradition," said Dory Gordon of Houston, Texas.

"It sends out a good message that the church is here for the world's people." Shops close to the Vatican sold out of "I love Papa Francesco" (his name in Italian) T-shirts.

In Argentina, people were excited to have one of their own become the leader of the Catholic Church. In the streets, people honked their car horns. This tradition is usually saved for when Argentina wins a soccer match. A thousand people gathered outside the Municipal Cathedral

A well-wisher holds up an "I love Papa Francesco" T-shirt as Pope Francis greets people after Easter Mass in Saint Peter's Square in 2013.

in Buenos Aires to show their respect. "As an Argentine and as a Catholic, the fact that the pope is Argentine is a huge joy," said Mercelo Alvrutin Suarez, who was taking part in the celebration.

To many people, Pope Francis represented a new beginning. He offered a chance to move the Catholic Church forward from the scandals that had consumed it. Yet people also knew that the new pope would not move the church forward in other ways. Pope Francis was very conservative—set in the old ways of the Catholic Church. That meant there was little chance he would change the church's stance on issues such as abortion, same-sex marriage, and allowing women to be priests.

A LETTER FROM THE PRESIDENT

When Pope Francis was elected, U.S. president Barack Obama sent his congratulations. In a statement released by the White House, the president said, "On behalf of the American people, Michelle and I offer our warm wishes to His Holiness Pope Francis. . . . As a champion of the poor and the most vulnerable among us, he carries forth the message of love and compassion that has inspired the world for more than two thousand years."

HOW WILL HE LEAD?

The night after Pope Francis was elected, he had dinner with his fellow cardinals to celebrate. He could have ridden to dinner in the official papal car. The "popemobile" is a Mercedes with white leather seats and a bulletproof glass enclosure to protect the pope. Instead, he chose to ride a bus with the other cardinals. He also refused to sit on a high platform at dinner. "So he greeted each of us as brothers, literally on the same level as we were," said Cardinal Dolan. At dinner, Pope Francis joked with the cardinals about his election. "May God forgive you for what you have done," he said.

Pope Francis's first day in his new job was a busy one. Early in the day, he returned to the church-run hotel where he had been staying. He wanted to pay his bill himself, even though he did not have to do so. "He was concerned about giving a good example of what priests and bishops should do," said a Vatican spokesman. The new pope also wanted to thank the staff who had taken care of him during his stay. Pope Francis greeted every one of them by name. The new pope even took time to call a newspaper seller in Buenos Aires to cancel his subscription. The pope thanked the shocked newspaper seller and sent his best wishes to the man's family.

Then he gave his first Mass as pope to a congregation at the Sistine Chapel. He read the Mass in Italian—unlike Pope Benedict, who had delivered his masses in Latin. During his homily, Pope Francis urged the church to stay true to its core faith. He also asked it to provide needed services to

Pope Francis *(third from right)* leads his first Mass as pope at the Sistine Chapel in Vatican City.

its communities. "In these few days, every symbol, every gesture has been, 'I'm here as a servant among you.' And people find that incredibly appealing," said Greg Burke, a senior communications adviser at the Vatican.

On Tuesday, March 19, the new pope was inaugurated during a Vatican City Mass. Up to one million of his faithful followers came to Saint Peter's Square for the ceremony. Heads of state arrived from all around the world. U.S. vice president Joe Biden (who is Catholic) was there. So were dignitaries from Latin America and other European countries. There were even members of other religions. Pope Francis has especially good relations with Jewish leaders. In

Pope Francis makes his way through a sea of flags and faithful Catholics as he arrives at Saint Peter's for his inauguration on March 19, 2013.

1994 he had helped the Jewish community in Buenos Aires after a Jewish center there was bombed.

One thing the new pope still had not done was meet the man who came before him. On March 23, Pope Francis flew by helicopter to Castel Gandolfo. Pope Benedict had been living at the hilltop castle in southern Italy since he had stepped down from his position in February. (He has since moved back to Vatican City, where a small monastery was renovated for him to live in.) The church said it was the first time a current and a former pope had had such a meeting. The two men prayed side by side, met in the castle library, and then shared lunch.

A week later, the pope again made news. He washed and kissed the feet of about a dozen prisoners at a youth

Pope Francis *(left)* and Pope Benedict XVI pray together in a chapel at Castel Gandolfo in March 2013.

detention center in Rome. It was similar to what he had done for people with HIV in Buenos Aires many years before. And it mirrored what Jesus had done many centuries before when he washed his disciples' feet. The act echoed Pope Francis's desire to help people who are poor or forgotten.

As Francis began his first week as pope, he had a big task ahead of him. Many Catholics were moving from

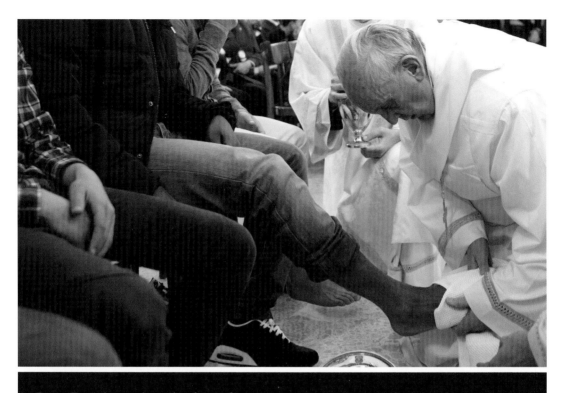

Pope Francis washes the feet of a young woman at a youth detention center in Rome.

the Catholic Church to other churches. The challenge was especially great in Latin America—the region from which the pope had come. In Argentina more than two-thirds of the people describe themselves as Catholic. Yet fewer than 10 percent regularly attend Mass. The Catholic Church was also very divided over the scandals that had shaken it. It needed a new beginning. Would Pope Francis be able to move the church forward? Or would he get caught up in the past? Could a man who still used a typewriter and followed soccer games on the radio modernize the Catholic Church?

"It remains to be seen whether he is a person of the 21st century or the 17th century," said Donna Doucette, executive director of the Catholic group Voice of the Faithful. Others were more confident that the new pope was the best choice to lead the church into the future. "This is a new breeze of fresh air that is blowing through the Church and the name of that breeze is Francis," said Cardinal Leonardo Sandri of Argentina.

Pope Francis blesses a huge crowd in Saint Peter's Square on Easter Sunday in 2013.

IMPORTANT DATES

1936   Jorge Mario Bergoglio is born on December 17 in Buenos Aires, Argentina.

1957   At the age of twenty-one, he becomes sick with an infection and part of his lung is removed.

1969   He is ordained as a priest of the Society of Jesuits, an order of the Catholic Church.

1973   Father Jorge serves as superior of the Jesuit province of Argentina. He holds this post until 1979.

1976   A brutal military junta takes over the government of Argentina. Father Jorge is blamed for not speaking out against them.

1979   Father Jorge serves as rector of Colegio Máximo San José in San Miguel, where he had studied earlier.

1992   He becomes the auxiliary bishop of Buenos Aires, assisting the archbishop.

1998	He becomes Archbishop of Buenos Aires.
2001	Pope John Paul II makes Jorge a cardinal.
2005	Cardinal Bergoglio is elected president of the Bishops' Conference of Argentina. He also receives the second-highest number of votes in the papal conclave. The conclave elects Cardinal Joseph Ratzinger as pope.
2013	Cardinal Bergoglio is elected pope.

SOURCE NOTES

9   Raf Sanchez, "Jorge Mario Bergoglio Elected New Pope: As It Happened," *Telegraph* (London), March 13, 2013, http://www .telegraph.co.uk/news/religion/the-pope/9928295 /Cardinals-meet-to-choose-new-Pope-live.html (March 19, 2013).

9   Philip Pullella and Barry Moody, "Argentina's Bergoglio Elected as New Pope Francis," *Reuters*, March 13, 2013, http://www .reuters.com/article/2013/03/13/us-pope-succession -idUSBRE92808520130313 (April 19, 2013).

16   Helen Popper and Karina Grazina, "Argentina's Pope Stood Up to Power, but Has His Critics," *Reuters*, March 14, 2013, http:// www.reuters.com/article/2013/03/14/us-pope-bergoglio -idUSBRE92D16J20130314 (April 19, 2013).

17   Jonathan Watts and Uki Goni, "New Pope's Role during Argentina's Military Era Disputed," *Guardian* (London), March 14, 2013, http://www.guardian.co.uk/world/2013/mar/15 /pope-francis-argentina-military-era (April 19, 2013).

20   Howard Chua-Eoan, "Pope of the Americas," *Time*, March 25, 2013, 18–21.

21   Rosie Hilder, "'Huge Heart': New Pope Preaches Church's Core Values with Compassion, say Argentinians," *Fox News*, March 17, 2013, http://www.foxnews.com/world/2013/03/17/huge -heart-new-pope-preaches-church-core-values-with-compassion -say/ (April 19, 2013).

22   *Aleteia*, "Jorge Cardinal Bergoglio Is Pope Francis: His Bio," March 15, 2013, http://www.aleteia.org/en/religion/news/cardinal -jorge-mario-bergoglio-is-pope-francis-480004 (April 19, 2013).

22   Emily Schmall and Larry Rohter, "A Conservative with a Common Touch," *New York Times*, March 13, 2013, http://www .nytimes.com/2013/03/14/world/europe/new-pope-theologically -conservative-but-with-a-common-touch.html (April 19, 2013).

26 Cavan Sieczkowski, "Pope Francis against Gay Marriage, Gay Adoption," *Huffington Post*, March 13, 2013, http://www.huffingtonpost.com/2013/03/13/pope-francis-gay-marriage-anti_n_2869221.html (April 19, 2013).

26 Schmall and Rohter. "A Conservative with a Common Touch."

28 *Week* staff, "Catholics in Crisis," *Week*, April 30, 2010, http://theweek.com/article/index/202388/catholics-in-crisis# (April 19, 2013).

29 Stephan Faris,"New Pope Shows Eye for Symbolism," *Time*, March 16, 2013, http://world.time.com/2013/03/16/new-pope-shows-eye-for-symbolism/ (April 19, 2013).

30 Chua Eoan, "Pope of the Americas," 10–21.

31 Amy Davidson, "We Have a New Pope: Cardinal Bergoglio Is Pope Francis," *New Yorker*, March 13, 2013, http://www.newyorker.com/online/blogs/closeread/2013/03/we-have-a-new-pope.html (April 19, 2013).

31 Holly Yan, "5 Things to Know about the New Pope," *CNN.com*, March 17, 2013, http://www.cnn.com/2013/03/14/world/pope-5-things/index.html (April 19, 2013).

31 Erin McClam, "Meet the New Pope: Francis Is Humble Leader Who Takes the Bus to Work," *NBCNews.com*, March 19, 2013, http://worldnews.nbcnews.com/_news/2013/03/13/17299920-meet-the-new-pope-francis-is-humble-leader-who-takes-the-bus-to-work?lite (April 19, 2013).

31–32 Alastair Jamieson and Claudio Lavanga, "Pope Francis Celebrates First Mass, Emphasizes Gospels," *NBCNews.com*, March 14, 2013, http://worldnews.nbcnews.com/_news/2013/03/14/17307513-pope-francis-celebrates-first-mass-emphasizes-gospels?lite (April 19, 2013).

33 Hilder, " 'Huge Heart': New Pope Preaches Church's Core Values."

33 Sanchez, "Jorge Mario Bergoglio Elected New Pope."

34 Jamieson and Lavanga, "Pope Francis Celebrates First Mass."

34 Ibid.

34 Ibid.

35 Faris, "New Pope."

39 Mary Wisniewski, "New Pope Must Deal with Divided Church in United States," *Salt Lake Tribune*, March 14, 2013, http://www .sltrib.com/sltrib/lifestyle/56004470-80/church-catholics-pope -catholic.html.csp (April 19, 2013).

39 Tom Heneghan, "New Pope's Simple Style Shifts Tone from Benedict's Papacy," *Reuters.com*, March 19, 2013, http:// in.reuters.com/article/2013/03/19/pope-style-contrast -idINDEE92I0AG20130319 (April 19, 2013).

SELECTED BIBLIOGRAPHY

Associated Press. "Jorge Bergoglio: Who Is the New Pope?" *CBSNews .com*. March 13, 2013. http://www.cbsnews.com/8301-202_162 -57574147/jorge-bergoglio-who-is-the-new-pope/ (April 19, 2013).

Barooah, Jahnabi. "White Smoke at Sistine Chapel Indicates Pope Election." *Huffington Post*, March 13, 2013. http://www .huffingtonpost.com/2013/03/13/white-smoke-at-sistine-chapel -indicates-pope-election_n_2866095.html (April 19, 2013).

Chua-Eoan, Howard. "Pope of the Americas." *Time*, March 25, 2013, 18–21.

Lackey, Katharine. "Key Facts about the New Pope." *USA Today*. March 16, 2013. http://www.usatoday.com/story/news/world/2013/03/10 /cardinal-jorge-mario-bergoglio/1976847/ (April 19, 2013).

Schmall, Emily, and Larry Rohter. "A Conservative with a Common Touch." *New York Times*. March 13, 2013. http://www.nytimes .com/2013/03/14/world/europe/new-pope-theologically-conservative -but-with-a-common-touch.html (April 19, 2013).

Suarez, Ray. "A New Pope, and Maybe a New Era." *PBS NewsHour: The Rundown*. March 14, 2013. http://www.pbs.org/newshour/rundown /2013/03/a-new-pope-and-maybe-a-new-era.html (April 19, 2013).

Yan, Holly. "5 Things to Know about the New Pope." *CNN.com*. March 17, 2013. http://www.cnn.com/2013/03/14/world/pope-5-things /index.html (April 19, 2013).

FURTHER READING

BOOKS

Behnke, Alison. *Pope John Paul II*. Minneapolis: Twenty-First Century Books, 2006.

Brennan, Gerald T. *The Man Who Never Died: The Life and Adventures of St. Peter, the First Pope*. Manchester, NH: Sophia Institute Press, 2005.

Keene, Michael. *The Catholic Church: Belief, Practice, Life, & Behaviour*. London: Folens, 2006.

Mancini, S. G. *Who Is the Pope? A Very Short Book for Children*. Seattle: Amazon Digital Services, 2013.

Stanley, George E. *Pope John Paul II: Young Man of the Church*. New York: Aladdin, 2005.

Wheeler, Jill C. *Pope John Paul II*. Edina, MN: Abdo Publishing, 2003.

WEBSITES

Argentina
http://www.turismo.gov.ar/eng/menu.htm
Travel through the beautiful country of Argentina—Pope Francis's homeland—with this tourism website. The site is translated into English. It features the country's most famous attractions, from sports to natural wonders.

The Jesuits
http://www.jesuit.org
Learn about the history of the Society of the Jesuits. Also find out what kind of work Jesuits are doing around the world today.

Pope Francis
http://ncronline.org/feature-series/pope-francis
The *Catholic Reporter* has its own website devoted to Pope Francis. It includes all the latest news about the Pope and the Vatican.

The Vatican
http://www.vatican.va
This is the official website of the Vatican. It includes a biography of the Catholic Church's new leader, Pope Francis. There is also information about past popes and the church in general.

Vatican News
http://www.news.va/en
Find out what is going on in the center of the Catholic Church with this news site from the Vatican.

INDEX